Lucid Dreaming

The Ultimate Guide On How To Literally Make Your Dreams Come True

(Controlling Your Dreams For Better Sleep And Creativity: Essential Knowledge)

Alejandro Thompson

TABLE OF CONTENT

Total Your Dream Recall 1
What Does Lucid Dreaming Mean? 20
Awareness 30
Lucid Dreaming's Advantages 33
The Significance Of Dreaming 46
What Is Lucid Dreaming? 59
Lucid Dream Control 64
The Advantages Of Lucid Dreaming 82
Keeping Your Dreams In Mind 97
Characters And Events In Dreams. 107
The Dream 128

Total Your Dream Recall

To enhance dream lucidity, begin with recalling your dreams. Journaling will be useful here. Place a notebook alongside your bed and jot down all the details you remember as soon as you wake up from a dream. The more awake you are after dreaming, the less you recall. They lose their color fast, act promptly for the best results.

We have multiple dreams during our 100 minutes of sleep. At times, the dreams may follow a common theme, while other times they may lack coherence and flow. To achieve lucid dreaming, practice remembering one clear dream each night. This step enhances self-awareness and aids in recalling lucid dreams upon occurrence.

Lucidity is more likely when one is self-aware.

Here are four tips to remember your dreams regularly. The more often, the superior. You dream even if you can't recollect them. A few with the rare sleep disorder don't dream.

Get enough sleep as step one. Stating the obvious, but important nonetheless. Your brain focuses on NREM during initial 4-6 hours of sleep. This is where the body can rest and repair itself. You will dream briefly during this period. It's difficult to understand what's happening and there's not much to remember.

After NREM, comes REM sleep, where the mind processes emotions and undergoes psychological repair. The highest chance for lucid dreaming occurs during REM. If you lack sufficient and consistent sleep, you will have trouble achieving lucid dreams due to reduced dream frequency. Lack of sleep harms your mental and physical health and decreases your chances of having lucid dreams. Strive for eight hours of sleep. You'll experience positive feelings and achieve lucid dreaming.

The subsequent action is maintaining a dream diary, as previously noted. When you start getting sufficient REM sleep, record your dreams actively. Maintain an illustrated and written journal, regardless of your level of artistic prowess (my own artistic ability is limited to stick figures). At times, it can be hard to articulate a visual or experiential encounter. Draw it up!

Write or draw in your dream journal during the initial five to ten minutes after waking up. Record all the details you recollect. Unpolished or incomplete is permissible. The sooner you record the details, the preferable. Underline unusual symbols, scenes, emotions, or people for special note-taking. Write in present tense for best results. Write as if the dreams are occurring to enhance lucidity, despite the fact that they have already happened in the past.

I want to bring up a dream recall experiment before proceeding to the next step. Requires dedication, but definitely rewarding. Your task sounds insane. Align your waking time with your REM sleep by ending your sleep cycles. When we wake up directly from a dream, our recall of things becomes much clearer, as per studies.

The costless approach is to schedule your phone to wake you up after 4.5 to 5 hours of sleep. Hopefully, you'll wake up during your initial phase of REM sleep. Jot down your morning recollections promptly.

Set your alarm to ring every ninety minutes throughout the night. If you usually take time to fall asleep, add an extra ten to twenty minutes to your bedtime accordingly. Try this on a non-work night for better results. You might feel tired due to the interrupted sleep. Still a valuable experiment to attempt for achieving lucidity.

Another way is to utilize a Fitbit. This product is low-priced (with Flex or One models) and records sleep patterns when synced with your phone. You can also set a silent alarm to avoid disturbing your partner, pets, or children while you experiment at night. The Neuroon sleep mask is a newer option for monitoring your sleep. It's highly advanced and capable of EEG-like brainwave monitoring. It employs sound and light as cues to indicate lucid dreaming, aimed at fostering self-awareness during the dream state. Neuroon costs around three-hundred dollars, while Fitbit One and Flex are priced at approximately ninety-nine and one-hundred and twenty dollars respectively.

The objective of the sleep experiment is to remember five, vivid dreams. You may be amazed by the quantity of dreams you have every night once the experiment is completed. Don't repeat this experiment frequently or consecutively for multiple nights. Frequently interrupting your sleep at night can have negative effects on your health.

Step three in dream recall involves taking B6 supplement. A 2002 double-blind study found that 250mg of B6 per day led to a rise in dream content. This involved heightened vividness, intensified emotions, brighter colors and oddness. You only need 100mg per day to obtain this. Begin with a small amount and gradually increase until you find your suitable dosage. Consult your healthcare provider before taking this supplement to avoid potential medication interactions. We want to ensure that we are promoting your health.

Those steps are crucial in recalling dreams. Any order works, or you may prefer one or two. You have the freedom to decide whether or not to use a vitamin or supplement. Keeping a dream journal is the best way to increase your chances of lucidity.

Lucid is a guide that exposes how you have manifested the things you dislike in life, rather than being a book on dreams. We must adapt and evolve, as sentient beings, throughout our life cycle. We must acknowledge that we are sleepwalking through our greatest earthly seasons.

I have awakened many individuals from their mental resting state through my teachings on this journey. Tina was among them. Tina appeared successful outwardly but lacked self-respect for her accomplishments.

Tina shared with me her experience of speeding while running late for work, feeling slyly unnoticed. "I haven't been caught for speeding this morning and I believe I'll have a smooth ride to the office," she said. Tina's mother and daughter Megan were the only issues during her commute due to her mother's tendency to be a back-seat driver.

Tina felt lucky to have made it on time through traffic, despite the warning from her boss the day before. He warned Tina, "Be punctual or you'll lose your job!" Tina's mother cautioned her to slow down while narrating. Tina, consider safety when driving with Megan. I know mom, I know. "Your driving will lead to a fatal accident," her mother warns. Mom, not now, I'm running late.

You're consistently tardy, love, even on your wedding day. She recalled the conversation with her mother that led to her daughter waking up. She thought if she could reach the next exit, she'd be at her desk in less than five minutes.

While answering her cell phone from the center console, Tina was alerted by flashing lights and sirens. She hoped the trooper wasn't aiming for her with her mother in the car. He followed her and told her to stop, as she anticipated. She exclaimed 'dammit, I knew it!' as her heart pounded outside her chest.

I was aware this would come and it will be expensive. She recalled her past, realizing she had pushed the boundaries for extended periods. She believed that this incident would result in losing her job, missing a mortgage payment, and further damaging her already-strained marriage. Tina's mother's teachings were about to be realized.

Tina's life was not going according to her plan. She considered the possibility of persuading the officer to let her off the hook, if he was amicable. Perhaps I could persuade him to give me a warning instead of destroying my career. "I didn't kill anyone," Tina mutters to herself. The patrol officer had a stoned expression, indicating to Tina that there would be no future breaks.

Tina's strategy now involves staying low-key and playing calmly. She suddenly exclaims, 'God! I wish I could relive my life again.' There are no do-overs in life, and hindsight is always 20/20. During such times, the channel between the conscious and subconscious mind is unobstructed.

She remembers multiple outstanding parking fines and her insurance has expired. She abruptly turned and spoke to the officer in his crisp uniform, visible through the rain-spattered window on the left. Guilt-ridden and unsupported by her mother, Tina grew increasingly agitated about her unfulfilling life. Tina's bloodstream was flooded with cortisol and epinephrine due to the release of her body's stress chemicals.

Tina's mother tried to console her frustrated daughter, but Tina flinched in a protective response. Tina screamed loudly and woke up from her nightmare. Did I forget to mention it was a nightmare she described to me?

Tina sat awake on her bed's edge, surrounded by crumpled, sweaty sheets. She realized it was a nightmare. She was grateful that it wasn't her current reality. She prefers her current life despite the difficulties, to the one she just imagined.

Tina was unaware that this would become her reality after two and a half years.

Tina could have prevented problems if she had analyzed the clear message to her unconscious mind. She could have achieved her childhood dreams if she had acted on her premonition. If she had questioned why her estranged mother was warning her about her personal matters, what would happen?

Upon awakening, her recollection of the dream faded from her consciousness. Is she listening to the confirmation of her disordered life in her dream-like state?

The unconscious mind's message is more powerful than the conscious brain's. The unconscious mind communicates lessons through dreams and nightmares to avoid confusion.

In the subconscious state, we use 95% of our brain's capacity to learn, process and release daily stressors. During wakefulness, our mind functions at only five percent of its full intellectual potential, resulting in lesser memory recall compared to when we are asleep.

To achieve lucidity in daily life, improve your brain's ability to let go of emotional distractions from daily trivial matters. Anyone can develop their ability to be aware and in control of their thoughts without requiring guru or monk status.

Your potential to attract happiness, wealth, and the right people has been in your unconscious mind since you were six. This book will improve your ability to see clearly by unloading information from your crowded mind, rather than adding new knowledge.

Daily encounters reveal people's falsity. Their innate abilities remain latent in their subconscious. If they are passive in their lucid unconscious mind, they may appear to be tough when awake. Strong-willed individuals may behave gently around others during their lucid unconsciousness to avoid intimidating them.

In Tina's dream, I showed you a woman who couldn't win her mother's approval. I assisted her in breaking her cycle of blame until that day. Tina's mother's image and negative criticisms haunted her continuously.

Tina's dreams often portrayed her mother and other influencers as enemies or monsters. Her mom was a back-seat life driver in one of her last dreams, as I had told you. But, these images distorted her initial caregiver into a more domineering figure than reality.

Tina's subconscious makes her a passive person who wakes up with a negative attitude every day. At work, she displays a protective and controlling attitude towards others. She maintains control and expects acknowledgement from those around her.

Tina has unknowingly become the kind of mother she used to criticize to her friends. To discover her authentic self, she needs to embrace her inner childlike nature prior to adopting a defensive persona. Her answers lie only in her dream or nightmare.

In dreams, valuable secrets and life-saving innovations are revealed. Unconscious dreams and nightmares have aided medical cures, sustaining humanity.

Most of these ideas were conceived by ordinary people like you, who integrated their subconscious discoveries into their conscious minds. Your future is brighter than your past. Imagine that your dreams are created by chemical reactions in your brain, rather than your eyes seeing images.

People who have cultivated conscious lucidity have used their intuition to preempt potential harm and chaos. They have overcome poverty to become wealthy, and despair to attain happiness. Consider some inventors influenced by dreamlike states.

What Does Lucid Dreaming Mean?

We are unaware that we are dreaming while asleep. Our dreams can sometimes feel like reality. We realize it's a dream only after waking up.

Controlling our dreams is difficult because we usually don't realize we're dreaming. People tend to dream about their recent memories before sleeping.

We can be completely ignorant of our dream content. We can become aware that we are dreaming while we are still asleep. The term for being conscious of our dream state during a dream is known as lucid dreaming.

Stephen LaBerge, from Stanford's Sleep Research Center, studies lucid dreams and describes them as "being awake in your dreams" and "dreaming while fully conscious."

Lucid dreaming starts when we encounter something too strange to be real. When you dream of an embarrassing scenario like attending school bare, you may doubt its reality. If you find yourself questioning why you're naked in a dream, it's because that scenario seems abnormal and implausible, and it may lead you to the realization that you are, in fact, dreaming.

Most of us don't experience this regularly. We may ignore the unrealistic details in our dreams and fail to realize that we are dreaming.

Lucid dreaming means realizing that you're dreaming while you're dreaming. Lucid dreaming does not guarantee complete dream control. You can train your mind to recognize and control your actions in a dream.

Dreamers enjoy several benefits from lucid dreams. Chapter 3 will cover the advantages of lucid dreaming. Although not everyone experiences lucid dreaming, we can learn how to have lucid dreams. Chapter 3 will discuss methods for achieving lucid dreams.

Techniques for promoting Lucid Dreaming.

I

Can one LEARN lucid dreaming?

To induce a lucid dream, be more mind than body. To become aware of the space density surrounding you, focus and observe your environment.

You must transition from thinking to feeling.

When thinking, the mind mainly focuses on managing and processing emotions. Your thoughts are experiences from the external world that have been internalized. This was termed the reality principle by Freud.

Being in a state of feeling involves shifting focus from thoughts to physical sensations such as pain, warmth, comfort, fear, anxiousness, and happiness.

DREAM JOURNALING

Lucid dreams require attentive observation of your dreams. Repeat the affirmation 'I intend to remember my dreams tonight' as your plan.

Have a dream journal and pen next to your bed to record your dreams immediately after waking. Jotting down notes can help you IDENTIFY your dream patterns more easily.

Do it upon waking. To record dreams effectively, act quickly. Dream logic is difficult to convey because it often lacks coherence when articulated to others.

What do you write in a dream journal?

Write using the present tense. Relive your dream in real-time and describe it.

It will aid in recording specific details for future reference.

Capture emotions, not just the plot. Make a habit of recording your inner emotions during dreams.

Did you feel nervous, embarrassed, or scared?

Did you recognize the setting?

Did the dream inspire you in any way?

Read through your dream notes after recording them for a few nights. You may observe recurring patterns or symbols.

Do you frequently have dreams involving barking dogs or elderly women appearing in unusual locations?

Dream analysis is an art more than a science.

Practice affirmations thrice daily as the second foundational habit.

To learn lucid dreaming, you need to give your brain an excess of positive reinforcement. Lucid dreaming chances rise with doing this minimum 3 times daily. Use affirmations to help remember your dreams and make progress. Recite them as if they've already occurred with a forceful tone. The words' intent and intensity matter most. Try loud, whispered, and silent affirmations.

Continue with the most effective approach for you.

Examples of Affirmations:

Recite your affirmations thrice daily, 11 times per session for a total of 33 repetitions. You are welcome to make one yourself.

I excel at lucid dreaming.

I value recalling every aspect of my dreams.

I am committed to mastering lucid dreaming.

Lucid dreaming mastery is my main goal.

Tonight, I will dream with clarity.

I lucid dream whenever I go to sleep.

Dreaming lucidly is easy.

I remind myself to perform reality checks frequently during the day.

I do reality checks in my dreams.

I possess the ability to recognize my dream state and achieve lucidity effortlessly.

I experience vivid dreams nightly.

I commit to mastering lucid dreaming in 100 days with discipline.

Recording Your affirmations

You can record your affirmations as an mp3, if desired. Speak with assurance and authority. Speak the affirmation as if it has already happened. Listen while sleeping or doing tasks. Run it on low volume in your earbuds all day to make it a subliminal affirmation. Recorded affirmations can be added to your favorite songs for an interesting use. Add affirmations to your playlist songs using an editing software. Create a subliminal affirmation track by making the audio of the affirmations barely audible.

Information Overload

To become skilled at lucid dreaming, you need to study it extensively. Read 1 book per week about lucid dreaming and its related subjects. Consume lucid dreaming podcasts and videos daily. Find individuals within your friend and acquaintance group who engage in lucid dreaming. Learn from them by observing their methods. Take notes. Airpods can be used to listen to lucid dreaming information while doing chores like grocery shopping. Listen to lucid dreaming info/affirmations whilst falling asleep. Learning rapidly in any aspect of life requires saturating oneself with information.

Awareness

It's similar to driving a car. You drive down the open road while observing the center line. You observe the clouds and road signs as you go. Your unconscious mind surfaces when your conscious mind is not overly stimulated. You experience serene concentration amidst the artistic freedom. A horn startles you back to reality as you realize you were daydreaming while driving. Timing is everything. You woke up at the optimal time to extend the dream experience, allowing you to expand and re-imagine it. To wake up in your dreams, shift attention and be fully aware to learn and create your dreams. We dream during waking and sleeping periods. Self-observation often accompanies awareness. Self-reflection is crucial for spiritual growth and awakening.

A dream in which you have consciousness of it is a lucid dream.

I founded DrainThatPain, a holistic technique for chronic pain elimination. I created the documentary 'DrainThatPain' during a year-long period, while commuting from Northern Virginia to Nashville, Tennessee. Lucid dreaming is like directing a movie in your mind's eye.

You can learn a lot about your mind. Your can accomplish that as you rest. Imagine the increased power of creating your dream reality if you intentionally and attentively managed your sleep.

Giftedness is not a requirement for lucid dreaming. All of us possess this skill. Intention setting allows for learning. You also dream at night like everyone else.

Reader, has boring dreams. As highly evolved mammals, we require sleep for our brains to process the vast amount of daily information from our senses. Brain consolidates and organizes memories in various regions. The unconscious mind's primary role is bodily protection. Early humans learned to evade Sabre-tooth tigers at night and heal from their injuries. Our dreams portray the same contradictions. The opportunities for self-learning are infinite. Simply set your intention to expand your awareness. Don't be afraid. The Shadow will never burden you with more than you can bear, as per Carl Jung. At first, you may encounter a situation that shocks and enlightens you. You'll learn to identify being in a dream and alter it from the inside. Hint. Forgiveness always works!

Lucid Dreaming's Advantages

Benefits exist for lucid dreaming. Let's explore the top benefits of lucid dreaming: Gain access to valuable information about yourself and life by summoning a jewel to answer your questions. You can acquire crucial.

Details on your innate abilities, unutilized talents, disregarded memories, untapped potential, etc.

Lucid dreams materialize the unconscious gem that solely resides in your mind. To enjoy the benefit of controlling your dreams, you must first learn to be aware of when you are dreaming and then learn how to manipulate them.

Provides total freedom for any action.

Every lucid dreamer desires to explore a unique aspect during their lucid dreams.

Lucid dreaming can help you control chronic anxiety or social anxiety disorders.

In a lucid dream, speaking to any audience size is effortless. You have the freedom to speak extensively before the United Nations General Assembly. By practicing this, you improve your public speaking skills and overcome your fear of public appearances.

Lucid dreamers have utilized their dreams to spend time with their celebrity crushes and engage in romantic activities.

In lucid dreaming, you can fulfill your desires like flying a private jet to stunning islands and marrying celebrities like Kim Kardashian, Brad Pitt, Jenifer Lopez, or Michael Jackson. This can be extremely gratifying and revitalizing.

Enhances Sleep Quality

Being mindful of your dreams during sleep leads to a serene slumber. Lucid dreaming and lucid sleep lead to optimal relaxation for high-quality sleep. You can achieve this by managing your sporadic nightmares and racing thoughts that disrupt your sleep and wake you up before sunrise. Lucid dreamers often report this benefit as one of the most common.

Improves Your Memory

Sleep significantly enhances the memories you form while awake. Your lucid dreams strengthen your episodic and semantic memories. Lucid dreaming enhances episodic memory, while deep sleep consolidates semantic memories.

Episodic memory enables skill acquisition and improvement. Semantic memory involves remembering important facts and personal experiences. Dreaming lucidly improves memory retention. This benefit is vital for students and young people as it enhances their ability to retain what they learn during the day.

Facilitates Acquisition of Skills

Lucid dreaming aids in acquiring and mastering athletic skills. Dreaming of scoring a goal activates similar neurons in the brain as actually scoring one on the field, as proven by researchers.

Lucid dreaming can improve your skills through athletic training. This applies to those involved in other activities like cycling, mountaineering, music, singing, acting, etc.

Through lucid dreams, you can improve your skills and techniques for real competitions by practicing in the optimal gaming and sports settings.

Aids in Coping with Phobias and Panic Episodes

Lucid dreams can help conquer height phobias rapidly. You can fly and skydive in your lucid dreams. Lucid dreaming allows you to have risk-free adventures.

In a lucid dream, you have the ability to manipulate your descent after jumping from the plane, controlling your speed, floating, and guiding yourself to a safe landing. Jumping off an airplane at approximately 10,000 ft has helped lucid dreamers with a fear of flying to conquer their acrophobia. Above sea level. All phobias follow the same principles, including ones for crowds, water, animals, speedboats, and more.

Now, let's examine easy and useful reality checks that aid in determining if you are in a lucid dream, after discussing some clear advantages of lucid dreaming.

Technique 1: Maintaining a dream diary.

To begin lucid dreaming, it's crucial to emphasize dream journaling as a useful method for monitoring your lucid dreams.

What is Dream Journaling?

Writing down your lucid dreams in a journal is called dream journaling. Dream diary is crucial for lucid dreaming as it aids in recording and recalling dreams easily. Write down your lucid dreams in a dream journal immediately upon waking. Include the date and time of the lucid dream in your recording.

Record every aspect of the dream, such as characters, sounds, colors, and your role. Ensure a detailed depiction of your dream through painting. After recording a dream, reflect on significant life events like promotions, marriages, or break-ups. This will aid you in recognizing the underlying reason behind your lucid dream and its intended message or objective.

To practice lucid dreaming, you must keep a dream journal as it is crucial. Start journaling your lucid dreams from day one.

Crucial Tasks for Writing in a Dream Journal

Besides keeping a dream journal, you must recall and apply key aspects for effective dream logging.

Experts recommend forming an emotional connection with the dream journal to boost the writer's interest in maintaining it. You should maintain consistency in your dream journaling. Adorn it or select a journal that attracts you.

Place Your Pen and Log near Your Pillow: Ensure that your pen and dream diary are within arm's reach of your pillow, allowing you to record your dreams quickly before forgetting them.

Name Your Aspiration: Provide a title to your goal. This will help you grasp the theme and message of it.

Capture morning dreams: Studies indicate five sleep cycles per night on average. REM sleep phase concludes every cycle. Dreams during this period are proven to be vivid by science. People dream for an average of 100 minutes every night and REM sleep is longer closer to the morning. Record your morning dreams as they are clearer at that time.

Reality Testing: also known as Reflection, is the 2nd Technique.

Reality testing, or reflection, is a commonly practiced form of lucid dreaming. Reflection is the act of contemplating and assessing the external world and your connection to it, used in psychotherapy.

Reflection aids in gaining self-awareness by analyzing and comprehending personal feelings, thoughts, emotions and behavior. Reality testing helps analyze and understand negative thoughts through behavior therapy and psychoanalysis, developed by Sigmund Freud.

Reflecting aids lucid dreaming by enhancing your comprehension of your thinking patterns. Let's talk about reality testing methods.

Reality Testing Techniques

You realize you're dreaming when you have a lucid dream. Dreaming while being aware that you are dreaming is called a 'dream initiated lucid dream.' When you enter a dream state directly from being awake, it is known as a 'wake initiated lucid dream.' Both types can aid in self-reflection and understanding of your thoughts, emotions, and feelings.

Here's what you need to do to practice reality testing and regularly engage in lucid dreaming.

Create a Dream Diary

Create a dream journal now if you haven't already. Write down your dreams upon waking. To recall a dream, focus on the scenes from your subconscious mind before waking up. This aids dream recall. Record your dreams in a journal and review them daily to enhance your dream recollection ability.

Be Aware

Be mindful while doing chores. Be attentive to your surroundings and closely observe everything when you do something. Watch for odd behaviors, surreal experiences, or peculiar ideas.

Develop awareness of your surroundings to train your mind to acknowledge it. This will enhance your level of mindfulness. This technique enables full mindfulness during dreaming, facilitating easier dream analysis. Take a note of any distracting thoughts during mindfulness practice and investigate their origin. By doing this, you can stop the thought from bothering you in the future.

Cultivate the Right Attitude

The right attitude is crucial for practicing reflection. Believe you are dreaming and question if it's real.

Periodically ask yourself 'Am I dreaming?' and perform a reality check.

Assume the answer to your own questions is 'yes'. By assuming and practicing this, you'll feel like you're lucid dreaming and be able to do reality checks. After asking yourself, perform a reality check.

Use Different Reality Checks

Perform these reality checks:

To perform the nose pinch reality check, use your finger to hold your nose and then pinch it. Breathe in through your nostrils instead of your mouth. You are dreaming if you can do it, but not if you cannot breathe via your nose.

Inspect your hands and feet attentively. If distorted, dreaming; if not, awake.

Read a page from a book and then avert your gaze. Glance back at it after a brief pause. Do it twice. Blurry text indicates a dream state, while stable text means you are awake.

Consistently performing reality checks trains your mind to do them in your dreams, leading to dream awareness. Practice reality checking effortlessly by following these steps patiently and with motivation.

The Significance Of Dreaming

Psychological Introspection

Freud saw dreams as reflections of our deepest sexual fears, desires, and anxieties. He proposed that taboo thoughts are disguised by the mind with absurd objects and images in dreams. Objects within a dream needed to be analyzed for Freud to understand its meaning.

Dreams exist for our benefit, according to the humanistic approach. The significance of dreams to humanists lies in how you respond to them. Dream behavior holds significant importance. Studying this conduct can assist in handling practical obstacles.

The behaviorist view of dreams proposes that external stimuli influence the content and manifestation of dreams. If your employer constantly pushes you to work hard and excel in your projects, you will probably dream of being pushed. Interpreting your dreams aids in preventing their recurrence and alleviating your waking dilemmas.

Dreams provide a chance to address unaddressed thoughts and emotions that are inaccessible during the day, particularly in busy schedules, according to the cognitive approach. Stress levels can go unnoticed until bedtime when the brain processes the day's discomfort, agitation, and frustration.

Ignoring a dream is ignoring the self, according to all these approaches. If you ignore your dreams, you may face challenges in self-confidence, self-respect, identity, and self-understanding.

I feel hungry, but it's not significant.

When did my feelings stop mattering? Your dreams matter, as do you.

Analyzing your dreams can aid in personal growth and self-healing. The above approaches and theories are interchangeable.

What themes did your last dream have? Were you fleeing? Did you watch the sunrise? What were you doing? What were your feelings on the matter? Were you afraid? Were you in awe? What is your current feeling about it?

At eighteen, I dreamt of cunning and malevolent "merpeople" encircling me.

I feared the merpeople might perceive me as a threat, despite being able to breathe while underwater.

My dream has themes of aquatic elements, fantastical beings, tribal culture, and seclusion.

To comprehend my thoughts during the dream, it is crucial to consider both the source and intensity of my fear. Drowning didn't frighten me. I had no fear of inadequacy. I feared not fitting in.

An understandable fear for eighteen-year-olds facing independence and the big world.

Recognizing the situation is just the beginning; the next step is confronting that fear.

I realized that not everyone will like me, so I controlled my fear of rejection. My self-liking suffices for my survival.

Trauma

Dreams can aid the recovery of individuals with trauma or PTSD.

Some wrongly believe that trauma is only experienced by war veterans or those who have been physically abused. This is untrue. Anything from a car accident to the loss of a loved one can cause trauma.

PTSD requires a minimum of two of these symptoms:

Nightmares

Vivid memories

Hypervigilance

Outbursts of emotion and physical actions.

Startled responses

Difficulty concentrating

I can think of three friends with undiagnosed PTSD. About 17% of college students have PTSD, according to a 2021 study by Aco Staff.

The fast-paced world and these statistics have led to an increasing interest in dreaming.

Exposure therapy principles can be applied in treating PTSD and trauma through lucid dream use. Gradual and secure exposure to one's worst fears is the basis of exposure therapy.

Overcome arachnophobia by gradually exposing yourself to spiders in a lucid dream. Managing fear enhances self-esteem and fear processing skills.

You can enter your dream, realize you're dreaming, and then confront your fear of spiders by interacting with your surroundings. You could give a giant spider a funny hat or purple kitten heels by using magic. Assign a personality to the spider. You'll befriend the creature and go on a galaxy tour together. A compassionate and interactive dream can alter your perspective on spiders.

Repetitive dreaming of this kind conditions the brain's perception of spiders. You start to acknowledge and value them.

Dealing with trauma involves the same approach. Identify your trauma to begin with. Trauma differs from depression as it has a distinct origin that can be recognized through emotions, nightmares, unconscious thoughts, and phobias. Identify your trauma to start working on it.

Contextual analysis of my mermaid dream can aid in understanding dream-based trauma healing.

At 18, I experienced bullying in school. Unfriendly mermaids chasing me represent my trauma and isolation.

Repeating the same dream nightly won't benefit me. I'll modify how the dream events unfold. I will prolong the vision and add a kinder conclusion.

To do this, I must plan ahead of past events. Escaping from the mermaids' enslavement alone won't heal my trauma. I want the ending I desired in reality to alleviate my trauma. In my dream's conclusion, the mermaids accept me or I retaliate against them.

My question is, 'What do I want?'

Your answer may vary, and that's fine. Choose what lets you sleep peacefully.

I am passionate and enjoy victorious battle scenes. I chose to conclude my aspiration by locating my spot among a group of killer whales. We went back to the mermaid cave and got our revenge as a team. The mermaids left, and the orcas and I peacefully coexisted until the end of our lives.

Expanding and revisiting this dream aided my self-discovery. I acknowledge my hatred towards those who mistreated me and desire for them to witness my contentment in their absence. I acknowledge the presence of unpleasantries in my being. It's okay to feel happy after revenge. That is human.

You must open your heart and mind to your true self, found during your unconscious state, to achieve acceptance.

I accept the ending I have created and go to sleep. I envision, command, and manifest it. From a nightmare to a heroic dream. That victory affects me both in my sleep and during my waking life.

Now, I can start my recovery, assured that I am a capable and confident person whom everyone loves. I am a capable and confident individual who can achieve anything she sets her mind to. I belong somewhere, I have friends, and my existence matters.

Stephen Aizenstat created dream analysis to ease trauma symptoms in survivors (De Borde, 2019). It's an effective method that encourages individuals to envision new possibilities and rearrange their trajectories. Trauma survivors regain control of their lives as producers and commanders, rather than remaining as victims. Don't be the victim of someone else's dream - join me.

Ideas and Success

One recalled dream has been the catalyst for numerous successful journeys of businessmen, scientists, and millionaires.

Stephen King, a renowned horror writer, stated that several of his works were scripts based on his dreams. He elaborates in interviews on his use of dreams as inspiration for his books. It fits, but I won't elaborate.

World-renowned electro-musician Richard D. James incorporated the sounds from his dreams into his albums. He has earned millions through his music.

Einstein may be the most famous visionary of our era. His theories stem mainly from the inquiries he made during his dream contemplation. He derived the theory of relativity from a dream about a fence-jumping cow (SVAdmin, 2021).

How often do you count animals as you try to fall asleep at night?

Einstein saw meaning in the scene. Rather, he contemplated the diverse perspectives of the cows on the scene and the reasons behind them. So, the theory of relativity came into being.

They achieved success by drawing inspiration from their dreams. Remembering one dream can determine your entire future.

Lucid dreaming is not only for idea generation. Lucid dreaming allows setting and achieving goals. The activity's idea is to devise and establish a plan. When becoming lucid in a dream, control should be exercised as the first task, such as selecting the sky's color or walking in a specific direction. At times, the goal may be significant, such as easing distress, gaining self-awareness, authoring a book, or resolving a mathematical equation. You can fulfill a goal in lucid dreams, frequently succeeding. You are in control and thus accomplish these tasks.

Visualize the sensation of achieving your objectives over and over again. Improving your planning skills boosts confidence, enhances self-esteem, expands creative thinking, and provides greater fulfillment.

Only a practiced dreamer can find the courage to pursue and share their dream, even if only a small part is remembered, like Stephen King. Stephen King, Richard James, and Albert Einstein often had lucid dreams. Practice gave them the courage to pursue their beliefs and desires, and take control of their future. Their dream worlds fueled their daily existence.

What Is Lucid Dreaming?

A dream where one experiences clarity and awareness is lucid dreaming. You know you are in a dream during a lucid dream. You are experiencing a dream-like state while awake. It feels like a dream come true.

In lucid dreams, you are in control of what happens. Instead, you decide. You have control over your actions in lucid dreams, but in non-lucid dreams, your behaviors and experiences follow subconscious patterns and impressions.

During lucid dreaming, you are the writer, director, actor, and audience in your own personal movie theater. You may select the film.

Scientific Evidence Supports Lucid Dreaming

Dreams that are lucid can be tested and replicated. It's a scientifically established natural event.

Despite the practice being common among Tibetan yogis and spiritual traditions, scientists remained skeptical for a long time.

New research suggests that lucid dreaming has characteristics of both a waking and dream state.

What's the Benefit of Lucid Dreaming?

Lucid dreaming enhances personal growth, accelerates progress, and boosts mental capacity.

It boosts your spirituality and brings lucidity and consciousness. You will experience less stress and more happiness, harmony, and self-confidence.

Your body during sleep has unique abilities to override limitations and access sources of creativity.

In a dream, meditation can lead to profound spiritual revelations. Transformation in the dream state is more potent than in the waking state due to the following reasons.

The process is transparent as there are no external disruptions to your mind's production of all elements.

Furthermore, the change is deeper and occurs on the energetic level (Yilü).

What Is Your Mission?

It's important to understand the reason behind your desire for something, whether it's a new skill, material possession, or relationship.

Without this understanding, you may lose drive and quit. So, you must identify your deeper goal.

Why do you desire to lucid dream?

What is your ultimate goal?

Would you like to unlock creativity and achieve happiness and serenity?

Would you like to explore your spirituality and achieve enlightenment?

Want to have fun trying out different things in your dreams?

Would you like to impact the world through the energy and enthusiasm bestowed upon you by lucid dreaming?

What's your objective?

Lucid Dream Control

Believe you can.

If you dream of standing on a cliff and needing to fly, believe in your ability to fly and do it. If you attempt to fly in your dream and your dream character cannot, you will fall. If you anticipate pain from the fall, you'll experience it.

You can make things happen in a dream if you believe in them and have confidence in yourself. This can help you overcome fear and make your dreams come true.

Begin a fictional journal.

To become lucid in dreams, you need good dream recall and a clear understanding of your fantasies. A fantasy diary fulfills both objectives. A fantasy journal can be simple or elaborate. Existence's purpose remains constant. Keep your diary and a pen nearby your bed at night. Upon awakening, initiate a dream review. Quickly document all details of your fantasies. Include maximum details! Read your journal entries and analyze every dream each morning. The more you jot down your activities at night, the more you'll dream about similar things. You may dream about anyone or anything, such as your sister, pet, the ocean, school, or snakes. Dream signs are recurring dream elements that can help achieve lucid dreaming. Your recurring dreams contain people, events, places, and situations that are present in your unconscious mind without your awareness. Identifying dream signs acts as landmarks in the dream world, aiding in achieving clarity.

Startle during daylight hours.

Material science can also feature in lucid dreams' imaginative landscape. Awakenings show if we are dreaming rudely. Begin this process by using simple wake-up calls in your conscious life. Toggle the light switch when entering a room. Be mindful and stay aware of your actions. Identify common rude awakenings to easily recognize them when you eventually achieve lucid dreaming.

My favorite way to be rudely awakened is to look at my feet and realize I'm held down by gravity. I know I'm having a lucid dream when I can easily levitate a few inches above the ground. Do ten reality checks each day to quickly achieve lucid dreams at night.

Repeatedly asking 'Am I dreaming?' will train your mind to ask the same question during a dream.

You can tell if you're dreaming or not by checking if the reality seems distorted and illogical. You may think it's crazy to question your consciousness, but your doubts will disappear after your first Lucid dream. Soon, you will experience a sudden realization in your dream and exclaim: "Wait, it's working! I am lucid dreaming!

Reflect twice daily.

Clear-headedness is crucial for successful Lucid dreaming attempts during sleep, as meditation fosters a healthy mindset. Mental well-being should be a priority for all individuals, as it impacts various aspects of life, including dreaming.

Reflect at a good time during your day and again 30 minutes before bedtime. This contemplation technique will help you be more intelligent during the day and prepare for your lucid dreaming efforts. Use dream-enhancing supplements.

Dream enhancing supplements can improve your REM sleep, despite the fact that this progression is not crucial for your well-being. Rest is where you are meant to dream. The greater your overall benefits, the greater your dream cycles' benefits.

Start by taking a daily multivitamin and supplement with magnesium, choline, and fish oil for improved brain function. Melatonin is a natural and effective sleep aid as well. Before taking any new supplements, consult your primary care physician if you have any medical conditions or are taking medication.

Mellowing is the act of calming your mind, whether expressed audibly or internally, just before sleep. Repeat the phrase "I will realize I am dreaming when I dream tonight" until you fall asleep. Ensure to associate your memory cue with the one mentioned above. The greater your connection to your practice, the more impactful it becomes.

Don't worry if you don't have a Lucid dream quickly. Following these rules increases your chances of lucid dreaming, but it is not guaranteed. The more effort you invest in achieving lucidity in your dreams, the more likely you are to succeed, as with most things in life.

Comprehending your imagination and its indications

Working with dream signs is another way to integrate with state checks in lucid dreaming. Similar to state checks, begin with using dream signs during daytime and later extend the practice into nighttime. It's a strategy for responding that can be done during the day and at night. Using dream signs means recognizing unusual events in the day and using them as triggers for reality checks. Clarify your experience by dispelling illusions. It is a type of lucid dream called a "fantasy induced lucid dream," where the dreamer uses the content of their fantasy to achieve clarity. We become aware of our dream state when we say to ourselves, 'That's strange, I must be dreaming.' The strangeness brings us to realization. Whenever something unusual happens during the day such as a fledgling hitting your window or a book falling off a rack, immediately ask yourself, "Is this a dream?" Ask this same question each time a peculiar event occurs. In dreams, we encounter various abnormalities like abrupt spatial shifts, peculiar gaps, or bizarre occurrences. We may be experiencing surreal situations like flying, seeing pink elephants or running into unpredictable dreamlike scenarios.

If we assume these, as usual, we are not lucid.

Many types of dream signs exist. Frail dream signs come first. These events are highly unlikely and only occur in dreams. It's strange but not impossible to see an unusual dog walking into your dream house. Solid dream signs include objects or occurrences that can happen only in dreams, like a chair morphing into a boat or flying without a plane. "Individual" dream signs are the most helpful. These are recurring elements that occur in your dreams, particularly in recurring ones. That's where you can utilize recurring dreams. Note down these exercises, circumstances, individuals, or items in your imagination diary and get to know them. When they reappear in your dreams, use familiarity to induce lucidity. Use his essence to recognize that you're dreaming. Dream signs and "dream topics" aid in achieving lucidity. Get familiar with your mundane subjects: the usual scenarios, narratives, personas, objects, and actions. Review your fantasy diary for repetitive topics. Use your dreams of being pursued or late for a plane as a cue to realize that you're dreaming. Wait, I've been in this situation before... Let me pause and reflect.

Keeping a diary for two weeks reveals patterns. You are near a fantasy sign. You might have a lifelong recurring dream symbol, such as a fear of snakes. Dream signs can fluctuate with changes in your life, such as getting a new boss, without prior notice. Highlight reoccurring themes in your fantasy diary such as a large manor, owls, your sibling Joe, the park, and shame. Maintain a list of these imaginary indications.

Identifying dream signs trains your subconscious to detect them when they appear. If you often dream about your former lover, use it as a cue to realize that you're in a dream state. Remind yourself before sleeping that seeing your ex means you are dreaming. Familiar recurring places, people, or subjects in your dreams can help you realize that you are dreaming.

Lucid dream initiation system tested autonomously, more potent when combined with others. Most members achieved record-breaking success in just seven days without external help.

A lucid dreamer is aware of the dreaming state and can influence the sequence of events in their dream. Science confirmed lucid dreams are real and identified techniques to increase their likelihood.

Dreaming preparation for lucidity.

Proper equipment is crucial for successfully achieving a lucid dream. You need a pencil and paper or notebook and the 'lucidity' app installed on your smartphone. This app wakes you up with an alarm and automatically shuts off to reduce movement.

Don't Try

Don't attempt lucid dreaming during your first week of trying. You should aim to sleep and wake up at consistent times each day. Get 7 hours of sleep minimum, but strive for 8 hours. Prepare a regular sleep cycle with an alarm during REM sleep. An erratic sleep schedule makes it harder to identify the timing of your REM sleep.

Keep a pencil and notepad on your bedside table this week to jot down any morning thoughts, feelings or dreams. Write down dreams promptly as human memory of dreams fades fast. The dream's details hold significant importance. Read your previous night's dream notes before sleeping to refresh your memory. Preparing your mind before sleeping aids in recalling and documenting more details about the same dream upon waking up.

Trigger - Hands

Count your fingers by habitually looking at your hands during the day in this preparation week. Remind yourself to count your fingers before sleep every time you naturally consider lucid dreaming, for consistent practice. Training your brain to perceive it as a normal occurrence can be achieved by doing it during the day in reality. This is the trigger you will use to become aware of dreaming. In reality, you have 10 fingers but in a dream, it may be difficult to count them and you may have a different number of fingers.

Don't Do This

Abstain from alcohol and mind-altering drugs during the preparation week. Alcohol disrupts sleep, inhibiting REM cycle at times. The mind is affected similarly by different psychoactive drugs. Cannabis may help in falling asleep, but it increases REM sleep, making it difficult to recall dreams.

Avoid sleeping with or next to your partner to prevent unintentionally waking each other up during the night or with your alarm in the morning. Utilize your spare bedroom to enhance your lucid dreaming. If you have no choice, don't worry; but do inform your partner that you plan to set an early morning alarm.

To download the 'lucidity' app, either wait until you have a regular sleep pattern or do it within the week. Don't move upon wake-up for better sleep; this app aids in this.

The WBTB Technique

I have tested various lucid dream techniques over the years. All of them primarily require waking up. I have practiced MILD, WILD, and FILD lucid dream techniques. The technique I present in this chapter combines all three methods, incorporating elements of each into a single approach.

What is WBTB?

It's time to learn about the wake back to bed technique and how to use it effectively after completing your first week of lucid dream preparation.

I consistently use this technique since I discovered it.

Set your lucidity alarm for two and a half hours prior to waking up.

As you prepare to sleep, mentally rehearse your desired actions or goals for your lucid dream. This is like flying, swimming, and breathing underwater for me. I chant the phrase 'I will fly when I jump' to myself. I prepare my subconscious mind for sleep by lying in bed before falling asleep.

Thirdly, sleep until your alarm wakes you up.

Remain still when your alarm rings. Enable automatic turn off for your alarm. Don't give in to the temptation of going back to sleep now. Keep your body still to aid falling back to sleep while keeping your mind active and awake. Breathe deeply four times, inhaling for 4 seconds, holding for 7 seconds, and exhaling for 7 seconds. After taking breaths, start repeating the mantra in your mind. Say 'I will fly when I jump' if you want to fly, which I suggest for beginners as it is fun. Repeatedly do this to experience a relaxed body.

You may begin to sense a loss of bodily awareness at this point. Sleep paralysis is normal and indicates progress towards a lucid dream. Stay calm and avoid getting excited when you are close to this stage of sleep paralysis. Stay calm and resume the 4, 7, 7 breathing method if you suddenly wake up. Being calm helps your mind generate clear mental images.

When visualizing, repeat your mantra and picture yourself bending and extending your legs to jump and fly once you start to see shapes or faces in your mind. Persist with visualization and maintain relaxation. You will eventually receive it. Visualizing and thinking about it decreases the chances of falling back to sleep.

To lucid dream, focus solely on a thought and avoid other thoughts that can make you fall asleep.

We need your body to sleep to convince your mind that you are sleeping. The mind receives a signal from the body to sleep.

Begin dreaming soon and remember to observe your hands and count your fingers. Count your fingers to realize you are dreaming. I woke up immediately after realizing I was lucid dreaming due to my excitement. It's fine if this occurs; attempt again the following evening.

When you become aware that you're dreaming, focus on bending your legs, looking down, and jumping.

Persistently jump, while attempting to lift and flap your arms like a bird. I achieved flight in my lucid dream by flapping my arms and hovering above ground - it felt incredibly fulfilling.

The Advantages Of Lucid Dreaming

We discussed lucid dreaming because it has numerous benefits. Here are the benefits of lucid dreaming and why everyone should do it, whether you're a beginner or have already been trying it.

Improving Your Life

It enhances your life and career effortlessly. It allows for the accomplishment of tasks that might otherwise be neglected due to time constraints or personal preferences. You can do it effortlessly with the skills you already possess. You can become aware in your current dreams. You can achieve lucidity using techniques that require little time and effort from you. Therefore, it should be done without any excuse. You can benefit from your dreams and apply them for personal growth.

Discovery of Self through an Avenue

Lucid dreams offer an interesting way to learn about ourselves, our minds, and perception. It's true, and it usually surprises many people. When you're in an invincible position, your fear disappears, and you can pursue your true desires without hesitating because the fear of failure vanishes.

Imagining can't compare to the mind's reality simulation; many try but fail. Thinking is different from experiencing through senses. Lucid dreaming yields realistic and tangible experiences. Your brain perceives that everything is happening.

Engaging with dream life fantasies expands minds to various possibilities.

Skill Acquisition

Lucid dreaming is popularly used for this benefit. It is utilized for practicing practical skills. For instance, improving your lifting technique at the gym would be a prime example. You cannot build actual muscles while performing that lift in a dream as there is no physical usage of muscles involved. You are not burning more calories, hence won't lose actual fat.

You recruit and fire the same neurons needed for the lift when practicing.

You can practice techniques and improve real-world abilities through lucid dreaming, which many athletes are currently researching.

This is an ancient technique, not a modern one, and that's what makes it shocking. This has been a centuries-old practice, with expertise in visualization and lucid dreaming. The research has improved the techniques significantly.

Lucid dreaming allows for real-life practice instead of mere imagination.

Better Sleep Habits

It promotes healthy sleep habits by increasing anticipation for sleep, which is the fourth advantage. We don't usually anticipate sleep unless we're extremely exhausted and require some relaxation. We anticipate relaxation during our free time, but often overlook the importance of sleep. We stay up late to avoid sleeping. We seem to be dreading the end of the day. Most of us would readily accept an offer to stay awake for our entire lives without requiring any sleep. I developed bad sleep habits, and ironically, I was guilty of it myself. My poor sleep patterns had developed from a reluctance to go to bed. Lucid dreaming solved the problem perfectly. I discovered an enjoyable and thrilling activity to pursue during my sleep, without actually being in a state of slumber. I have yet to complete anticipated tasks from my slumber.

I now had a valid motive to anticipate sleeping. I improved my sleep habits by taking care of my sleep.

Mood Improvement

Lucid dreaming can improve your mood as you wake up feeling happier. Waking up and feeling excited feels great. You desire to share and record them. You anticipate the next dream. Your next course of action? Often, you've progressed to some extent. Perhaps you attempted a dream control method, it was unsuccessful, but you still made some improvements from your previous attempt. All those steps, improvements, and experiences were thrilling. Afterwards, upon waking up, you feel enthusiastic, joyous, and eager for the day ahead. It's a great mood booster.

Removal of Bad Feelings

Lucid dreaming can alleviate negative emotions and enhance positive ones. Fear is a major negative emotion. Lucid dreaming helps combat fears. In a lucid dream, fear can be confronted without harm in a secure setting. The clear dream eliminates risks in its environment. In the dream, you have the power to banish fear and can wake up at will. You can confront your fear gradually in your dreams until you conquer it. In a virtual environment, possibilities are limitless.

Assuming you fear spiders, for instance. You won't find a thousand spiders to bathe with in real life, even if you desired. Extreme exposure is dangerous, so avoid it. In a dream, you can use dream control to fill the bath with spiders. In dreams, you can influence your subconscious and alter your beliefs by inserting suggestions.

You can implant suggestions to overcome fears in both dreams and real life, not just by facing them. This isn't limited to fears. Elusive dreams can aid in overcoming negative emotions.

Lucid dreams offer immense potential for therapy and subconscious reprogramming. Using lucid dreaming yields powerful benefits.

Memory Improvement

The next one is that it can serve as an exercise to improve memory. Emotions aid in better retention of information. Reading a paragraph in a book doesn't create profound, lasting memories. If an emotional experience teaches you the same lesson as the book paragraph, you'll remember it for life.

Neuroscience of Lucid Dreaming - Chapter 3

Controlling lucid dreams can offer unparalleled insight and strangeness. You become aware it's merely a dream as you doze off and begin to hallucinate. You can keep dreaming while waking up, with one key benefit. Your brain creates the reality you experience. After awakening like Neo in "The Matrix," you can now manipulate physical laws. You can exhibit superhuman powers such as stopping bullets, flying, and delivering powerful punches to defeat villains. There is no spoon.

Lucid dreaming is subjective. During lucid dreaming, certain parts of the prefrontal cortex show higher activation levels compared to regular REM sleep, as per research. The prefrontal cortex is responsible for memory recall and decision making.

People who have frequent lucid dreams show a larger anterior prefrontal cortex, related to higher levels of self-awareness, according to research. People who reflect on their thoughts and actions in daily life can easily control their dreams, as per researchers.

A study examined if individuals with high and low dream lucidity varied concerning their capacity to introspect and communicate their mental state.

All participants completed questionnaires measuring their control, intensity, frequency, and metacognitive abilities related to lucid dreaming, such as self-reflection and self-awareness. Also, the participants had brain scans during a cognitive monitoring activity. The study entailed two 11-minute trials where participants rated their thoughts on an internal-external scale. Thoughts oriented towards external factors, including visual surroundings and scanner noise. Internal thoughts involve recalling past events or planning for the future and are not connected to the immediate environment.

Subjects with high lucidity exhibit greater gray matter volume in the frontopolar cortex than those with lower levels. Lucid dreaming and metacognition share similar mechanisms, particularly relating to thought observation. This is supported by increased brain activity during thought monitoring in both high- and low-clarity subjects, with even higher activity in the high-clarity group. The neural aspect of their relationship had not been investigated before despite being assumed.

Controlling lucid dreams could be achievable by monitoring our thoughts during waking hours, as future research may indicate. Researchers are unsure why people experience lucid dreams despite new investigative approaches. A recent study discovered that brain activity during lucid dreams appears to be a combination of REM sleep and wakefulness.

Vagus Nerve: Your Body's Communicative Highway.

The vagus nerve acts as the body's superhighway, transporting data between the brain and internal organs, and controlling the body's response at rest. It begins in the brainstem and descends to the digestive system. It also links up with organs such as the heart, lungs, and liver. This nerve branches out to the neck and torso, responsible for functions like relaying sensory information from the ear's skin, controlling muscles for speaking and swallowing, and affecting the immune system.

The vagus nerve is the tenth cranial nerve. The vagus nerve is a pair of nerves coming from the right and left sides of the medulla oblongata, despite being referred to in singular.

Messages continuously travel through the vagus nerve. The brain directs the body during top-down travel. 80-90% move from body to brain.

The brain-body link is why anxiety can cause stomach upset, deep breathing can soothe the mind, and gut instincts can be felt in the head, heart, and stomach.

The name originates from the Latin term 'vagus' meaning wandering, due to its wide distribution and size, the vagus nerve is colloquially termed so.

The vagus nerve controls the parasympathetic system, which is responsible for rest and digestion, in contrast to the fight-or-flight response of the sympathetic nervous system. The vagus nerve instructs the body to reduce heart and breathing rates and enhance digestion during a stress-free state. Sympathetic system takes charge in pressure and causes opposing reaction. The vagus nerve sends sensory signals from internal organs to the brain for monitoring their functions. The Vagus nerve has a significant role in the lucid dreaming process as it is activated during the rest-and-digest phase when lucid dreaming occurs.

High vagal tone

When the vagus nerve is healthy, a high vagal tone allows for resetting after stress in a person. Additionally, it's associated with lower anxiety levels, improved mood, enhanced blood-sugar control, decreased risk of cardiovascular ailments and stroke, minimized inflammation, and better digestive health.

Low vagal tone

Age and chronic stress lower vagal tone. Your vagal resonance is low, making it difficult to deactivate the sympathetic nervous system. It's linked to increased emotional reaction, impaired objectivity, inability to suppress negative thoughts, and weakened memory. Low vagal tone indicates low resilience, making it difficult for you to overcome challenges and achieve new objectives.

Low vagal tone manifests as system-wide inflammation. The vagus nerve releases acetylcholine, which reduces inflammation in the body. Inflammation and its associated diseases thrive in its absence, such as heart disease and depression.

The vagus nerve is under scrutiny as a potential solution to high levels of stress.

Keeping Your Dreams In Mind

A dream journal is a valuable item you'll need. It's necessary. The journal must be READILY AVAILABLE upon waking. Memories could vanish just by walking from bed to desk and booting up your computer, especially at the beginning. I initially used a paper journal during my Lucid dream journey and it was effective. I couldn't jot down my dream recollections quickly enough after recalling them with greater frequency. I changed to a laptop with keyboard and now I utilize a keyboard-equipped tablet. Your dream journal should be convenient and user-friendly. Voice memos and speech to text have been successful for many. Experiment with different options to find your ideal choice.

Recording dreams improves dream retrieval. Record what you recall about your dreams immediately after waking up for efficient dream journaling. I can manifest as a sensation, hue, form, or picture. Jot down any data fragment you recall. Read what you wrote before sleeping. Recalling these memories prior to sleeping boosts dream retention.

Repeating phrases to yourself is the simplest way to begin if you struggle with recalling your dreams. Repeatedly affirm to yourself while falling asleep and during the day something similar to.

I wish to recall my dreams.

I wish I could recall my dreams.

I'll record my dreams upon waking up.

My dream recall is improving.

My sleep is filled with dreams every night.

Dream Recall Summary.

The first essential step is to recall your dreams. Enjoy this!

Try using self repeated statements to recall your dreams.

Acquire a convenient and user-friendly dream diary.

Record any dream details in your memory, including unclear sensations, forms, noises, or pictures.

Write down more details as you remember more of your dreams.

Read entries from dream journal before sleeping.

Relish Recalling Your Dreams

If you're genuinely interested in Lucid dreaming, you'll eventually develop a natural enjoyment of recalling your dreams after you start doing so. Enjoy reading your dream journal and exploring your dreams once you are certain of remembering them, as it will involve your subconscious mind more and strengthen your foundation. Your dreams will increase in length. The details will become more complex. You will remain a passive observer, but your experience will be enhanced.

Remembering my dreams improved the structure and logic of my dream interactions and conversations. The stories I participated in had more continuity. At this point, I began to discover more about myself. Some dreams were not pleasant, as they involved arguments and aggression. What caused these dreams within me? My aversion to being incorrect? Why argue with a dream character?

Your dreams are YOUR handiwork. Your attitudes, beliefs, and actions are mirrored in them. Work-related disagreements can influence the content of your dreams. You may gain more clarity on decisions you need to make. Dreams are therapeutical as they naturally process and resolve life's events. Don't obsess over the interpretation of dreams despite their significance; also, record them. No interpretation required. Let things happen naturally. Observe the emotions aroused by a bad dream. Why were you scared?

I recall having some unsettling dreams at this phase. I witnessed a city resembling Amsterdam getting bombed, resulting in buildings being destroyed by explosions. Debris was flying everywhere. People got trapped in debris. When I ran to seek help, every person I met would abruptly collapse with a loud "Crack" noise due to a sudden broken ankle. I woke up scared in my bed. I recorded my dream in my journal and reflected on it. I feared things falling apart. My business and life choices were crumbling. Don't obsess over dream specifics. The specifics are metaphors to help your mind grasp the emotion's frequency being mirrored. This unpleasant dream helped me recognize and work through unknown fears.

Do not fear your dreams. As we recall more dreams, understanding will come naturally. By being open to both positive and negative dreams, we allow ourselves to connect with a more profound aspect of our being. Dreams reflect our inner thoughts. Dreams depicting unwanted experiences may begin to be perceived differently. Just something that highlights our internal wounds.

There's nothing to achieve in this step. Once you can consistently recall your dreams, you may begin implementing reality checks, discussed in the next chapter. Exploring your dreams and lucid dreams can enhance self-discovery.

Summary: Enjoy Your Dreams' Recall

Engaging in your dreams increases self-awareness. Allow the process to unfold organically.

You are the architect of your aspirations. Analyze your present beliefs to comprehend the origin of the emotions aroused by your creation.

- Don't get hung up in the details of your dreams. Shift your focus to the emotions evoked by the dream.

Engaging in enjoyable dreams can bring forth natural conflict resolution.

Once you remember your dreams regularly, at least 2-3 times per week, begin including reality checks.

Characters And Events In Dreams.

In dreams, we may encounter any character. They can be strangers. They can be benign. They can be evil. They have the potential to be various characters. Sometimes they speak. Sometimes they're silent. Occasionally, they're short-tempered males pursuing you with black capes trimmed in red.

We're transitioning to sentient beings from objects. Not all dream characters are human. Cats, dogs, donkeys, or pangolins are all possible options. They might communicate with you in your native tongue, or they might not.

In the dreamscape, material laws don't hold. That's part of why it's appealing. An exciting break from reality, whether short and informative or wild and chaotic, is alluring.

Let's explore dream characters and our interactions with them. How to enjoy, modify and manifest personal preferences in them (e.g. like I did with Mr. "Get Off My Lawn").

Who Are These People?

LaBerge and Tholey studied the significance of dream characters and how dreamers interact with them.

Tholey observed that these characters existed in the dreamer's mind as autonomous entities, demonstrating thoughts and actions that were separate from the dreamer, albeit at a conscious level.

Dreamers believed in the reality of dream characters for thousands of years. They were believed to carry secrets and predict future events, warning the dreamer of either danger or positive news. The ancients believed these characters were spirits visiting from another realm.

Freud believed these characters were subconscious personality complexes or sub-personalities of the dreamer.

Subpersonalities in a multiple personality syndrome-like model could manipulate the dreamer's cognition and, sometimes, physical movements during fugue states when the dreamer loses touch with reality.

No scientific evidence supports Freud's claim. Interpret the dream characters as you wish for this book's purpose. No definite answer exists due to the absence of any empirical framework.

You can interact with the people/characters in your dreams if desired. Dreamers can inquire about their dreams and gain insight into their contents.

Characters in lucid dreams may originate from the same part of our psyche as those we converse with during our internal dialogs. Yes, we talk to ourselves frequently, including myself. We communicate with a part of us that exists in a distinct realm of our awareness. It's a matter of self-reflection. We use our internal thoughts to evaluate our lives. We can express frustration, doubt, and difficulty. That internal sounding board resembles the individuals we encounter in our vivid dreams.

Tholey and LaBerge found that characters in lucid dreams can behave unpredictably when questioned. A study participant once asked their dream character to use an unfamiliar word. The dreamer didn't know the meaning of the word, "orlog," uttered by the dream character. This Dutch word means "quarrel" or "squabble," and the lucid dream context had that emotional setting.

Some dream characters would convey strange or unpleasant information to the dreamer, as noted by Tholey and LaBerge. This indicates a reality that goes beyond Freud's theory of sub-personalities generated by the subconscious and appearing in dreams. What is a possible explanation?

It's uncertain if these characters signify Jung's collective unconscious, but they could link us to humans from previous and current eras. Do lucid dreams allow access to the vast knowledge stored in the subconscious?

Without reliable, empirical evidence, dream characters remain unexplained.

How can we learn about these mysterious 'beings'? How do we engage with them? Let's explore!

Visitor: familiar or unfamiliar?

Your dream character's arrival is always a chance for something. You can benefit from every character you encounter in your lucid dreams, regardless of their nature or familiarity.

Familiar faces can be encountered in a lucid dream. You'll recognize departed pets and other entities or representations of them. You can manifest these people in lucid dreaming when you're ready. Suppose you've already dreamt of a past acquaintance, family member or pet. A manifestation can bring closure and address previous dreams indicating a lack of it.

When you dream about people you know personally and bring them to life, you have a more tangible concept. There is no confusion about the intended person or pet for manifestation. This skill is a prerequisite to discovering unknown personalities. Be cautious with your thoughts at this point. Our lucid dreams can contain visuals that are linked to our thoughts due to the brain's intricate structure. That can be bad.

Let's consider unfriendly or hostile dream characters before proceeding.

Tadas Stumbrys from Vilnius University suggests an effective approach for handling menacing figures in lucid dreams in his article, Inner Ghosts: Encounters with Threatening Dream Characters.

German lucid dreamers found that 20% of their dream characters were unfriendly. The lucid dreamers resolved conflicts by fighting, flying away, or solving the issue. Frequent lucid dreamers were more likely to practice the last strategy.

Stumbrys infers that aggressive dream characters may emerge due to personal conflicts or mental health issues, as hinted by other study results. He advises resolving conflicts with unhappy campers to promote peace. Stumbrys proposes that psychological healing is achieved through that resolution.

Stumbrys' commentary adheres to the Freudian theory of dream characters originating from the dreamer's subconscious, but it's worth noting the lack of scientific explanation for this phenomenon. You can heal old wounds through lucid dreaming. In our dreams, we have a unique personal experience that cannot be replicated by anyone else except through storytelling. Still, the experience remains unshareable.

By achieving clarity, we allow ourselves to access our innermost being, which motivates us to give ourselves the gift of recovery. This art form involves more than just improving oneself for personal gain. During lucid dreaming, we can explore our inner edges and burn them away. Bleeding makes us vulnerable. We can strive for a sense of completeness and ease in our own being, despite any disagreements in our beliefs. The information informs and enriches the practice, providing a solid understanding for all.

The people who model hostility are at the forefront of the challenge it presents. We encounter a companion in the form of an adversarial or intimidating figure in our dreams. That traveler has a message for you. The aim of hostility and threat is to grab your attention and prompt you to respond to the message.

Be truthful while preparing for playful dreaming, based on your own interpretation. What's in your subconscious? It's time to leave since it's clear that you're not contributing to the rent.

To handle hostile dream characters that represent people we know, choose fight or flight. Flight is generally easier for beginners who may lack confidence in the agility and strength of their dream body. You are the dreamer, and the body is yours, but to fight your way out of a hostile encounter requires supreme confidence. This technique demands simultaneous attention to muscle sensations, tension that drives the fight, and hostile character.

My advice? Fly first, fight later.

I wish everyone could achieve lucid dreaming to resolve conflicts on a personal level. If Freud's theory holds true, facing our inner conflicts can lead to a more peaceful and harmonious life, affecting those around us. If the theory proves valid during your explorations, gain advantage. As discussed, you control the rules in your dream world.

Now, we await a voice from the archetypes that direct human behavior, specifically from Jung's. You will identify these archetypes as you begin your lucid dreaming journey. They connect with both living and deceased individuals you are familiar with. They appear as enigmatic guests. Knowing these 12 Jungian archetypes helps comprehend dream characters and their roles in lucid dreams. They hold the cultural knowledge of all human generations. They are icons of our subconscious self-knowledge, known to all.

12 Archetypes

Ruler

The Ruler's love extends beyond power. The ruler's purpose is to maintain power through control. That may not sound appealing, but the Ruler aims to bring prosperity to the family and community through responsible management.

Rulers possess a tendency to control and believe in the philosophy of 'doing things on your own to get the desired outcome'.

Rulers include Kings and Queens, monarchs, leaders, aristocrats, politicians, bosses, managers, role models, and paper pushers, within social structures and organizations. Rulers are ubiquitous, and their identification is apparent.

The Ruler often has an egomaniacal demeanor, evident in their withering gaze and upturned nose. The Ruler may visit you in a dream to impart a lesson about your sense of responsibility and control.

Creator/Artist

What you can imagine, you can achieve, as the Creator/Artist knows for sure. They hope their creations endure and find intended audiences.

Creators and visionaries have zero tolerance for mediocrity within themselves. The Creator/Visionary's quest for perfection can hinder her progress. Search for those who appear disheveled, unfocused, and unclear.

This character represents your creative potential and can help solve any troubling issue in your life.

The Sage

The sage's goal is to discover the truth, as only it can liberate humanity. The Sage is analytical and demands empirical proof for reality, with no tolerance for deception.

The Sage's excessive focus on details can hinder their ability to take action.

Search for a youngster, a senior citizen, your former math instructor, or a traditional healer. You'll gain valuable knowledge from the Sage, regardless of how they appear in your lucid dream.

The Innocent

Contemporary society romanticizes "innocence," however, within this archetype, it has a submissive and emotionally numbed quality.

Passive, the Innocent yields to life's flow. Innocents, while optimistic and faithful, are boring due to their lack of emotional tension and predictability.

The Innocent can manifest in anyone, particularly among acquaintances. Most of us are familiar with the Innocent and their disinterest in reality as portrayed by this archetype. Your older brother, The Innocent, could be living in your parents' basement, unaware that the house has been sold. Perhaps a friend overspending with credit cards beyond her income. This archetype is defined by being almost boneless and tedious.

The Explorer

The Explorer fearlessly dashes around the world, ready for anything. By investigating the world around them, The Explorer discovers their authentic self and true identity.

The Explorer avoids conformity, prioritizing authenticity and fulfillment. The Explorer archetype values immediacy and freedom, viewing the expectations of polite society as restrictive shackles.

The Explorer visits to remind you of your dreams, bucket list, and hopes for your children. The Explorer could be a familiar person, like a friend or family member, who you trust from the past or present. The Explorer may bring a message of discovering our authenticity and enjoying the freedom in the urgency of life.

The Rebel

The Rebel is coming, so fasten your seatbelt, Buttercup. This archetype is prepared for a fight. The Rebel seeks to break rules and join revolutions.

Don't anger him, or he might show animosity through his dream character. The Rebel avoids trivial matters. Systems can be restarted.

It's time to shake things up when the wild man pays a visit. You're aware of this fact, as this tough individual appearing in a lucid dream suggests that you apprehend it also. Answer the Rebel's call for transformative action.

The Hero

The Hero is a brave fighter, representing the victory of courage over fear. Losing a leg is insignificant to the obstinate, confrontational Hero archetype, just like the Black Knight in the movie "Monty Python's Holy Grail."

The Hero believes his prowess and fearlessness will save the world, carrying a huge chip on his shoulder. The Hero archetype combines narcissism with a noble intent to fight for what is right, making it significant. Truthfully, many of us desire to be heroes in some way.

The Hero motivates you in your lucid dream to be the best version of yourself when you feel incapable. The Hero ignores your excuses.

The Hero is both the Black Knight and the aggressive drill sergeant. If you're not nurturing your goals, The Hero will remind you when you're tempted to give up.

The Magician

The 12 Archetypes, like humans, have both positive and negative qualities. The Magician remains unchanged. The Magician aims to achieve her desires without any negative consequences, by having faith in her ability to shape her surroundings.

That's where the real magic of manipulation occurs. The Magician's seductive power and our own power can both be wrongly utilized. Despite that,

The Magician is both a healer and Shaman, providing relief to Gilead in times of scarcity.

The Magician's arrival suggests a potential need for healing, be it physical or psychological. This is seldom an informal visit. Be attentive to the archetype's presence in your dreams.

The Jester

The Jester ensures that you stay amused with his humor. The Jester always attends parties and dislikes seriousness. Everything's a joke.

The Jester can provide entertainment, but can also hinder productivity. The Jester lives life to the fullest, disregarding mundane responsibilities and embracing youth.

The Jester's appearance indicates you require more enjoyment or a break from your current lifestyle. The visitor can have any appearance chosen by you or him, thus make a careful decision if clown phobia is a concern. Be prepared, as The Jester will probably choose that appearance. Some jokes are not humorous.

Every Man/Woman

The ultimate desire of this archetype is to blend in with the rest of the world. Believing in human equality, Everyman/woman embraces mediocrity as it's the norm.

This archetype seeks to form connections with others in the community through various means. Every person fears being excluded when seeking social acceptance.

The Everyman/woman embodies familiar values that resonate with most of us, regardless of whether we actually practice them, and is empathetic and grounded in nature. The Everyman/woman points out red flags for you. Are you sacrificing your preference to fit in? Staying in a displeasing job due to social relationships with colleagues? Are you alienated by over-achievement? Every person could be appearing in your dream to remind you of your origin or path.

The Lover

Excessive love can causc The Lover to lose themselves in meeting the needs of others despite being a vital force that drives the world.

The Lover's world requires only love. The Lover's sole purpose and reason for existing is because of it's effect on his heartbeat. This archetype primarily desires love associated with intimacy and sensuality.

When The Lover appears, be it Jake Gyllenhaal or a bridge troll, the message is unmistakable. Love is either desired or regretted, as it comes and goes. This archetype brings warmth to help heal or clarify your desire for love.

The Caregiver

The Caregiver archetype embodies mission, love, and service without conditions. The caregiver can vanish into the demands of those they care for, similar to The Lover. However, being a caregiver is equivalent to willingly sacrificing oneself. Caregiver's self-centeredness and neglect of self-care is evident.

Helping others at the cost of neglecting ourselves harms our ability to keep providing help. The caregiver may appear in your dreams if you are overworked and need a break. The caregiver may be present to motivate you to do the volunteer work you have been delaying.

Lucid dreamers can create dream characters. The better you become at lucid dreaming, the more control you have over who you encounter in your dreams. Dream characters are particularly affected by this. When you're clear about your role and motivations in a dream, you're more likely to gain from the lessons shared by dream characters, particularly the Jungian archetypes.

The Dream

In ancient times, dreams were considered a means of connecting with spirits, including God, and were imbued with spiritual or mystical significance. Dreams were message carriers, never ignored. Some prophets received messages from God through dreams according to religious stories. God instructed Abraham to offer his son as a sacrifice in his dream. Joseph was informed of his skill as a dream interpreter. He explained the Kings' dreams. The Holy Scripts (e.g. The Koran) contain these stories.

Nowadays, most individuals will react with a smile when you share that you received a message from God or spirits in a dream. Common people think dreams are unrelated to spirituality or mysticism. Dreams are psychological in nature.

Freud considered dreams seriously as a psychologist. Carl Jung is a notable psychologist in this context. Freud believed dreams reveal hidden desires. When the conscious mind is at rest, the unconscious mind murmurs. This indicates the phenomenon of dreaming.

Dreams reveal our unconscious desires. Our thoughts and memories reorganize during sleep, causing dreams. Dreaming reveals the contents of our unconscious mind.

Dream perception has vastly changed from ancient times to today's psychology. In ancient Egypt, vivid dreams were viewed as a sign of being blessed with special insight. Dreaming was considered by Egyptians as the ideal method to attain spiritual messages, divine revelation, or interact with spirits. Spiritual view considers dreams as receiving while psychological view considers them as production. There are two main perspectives on the dream. One view is that dreams are obtained, while the other suggests dreams are made.

Dreams are a receiving process and cannot be discussed from a spiritual perspective. We lack knowledge and detailed explanation about the spiritual realm. There are no books discussing the interpretation of dreams from a spiritual or mystical perspective. It hinges on the dichotomous decision of belief or disbelief.

The psychology of dream explains that we unconsciously produce dreams. The dream materials exist in our unconscious or subconscious mind. Our minds do not receive any message to interpret from the external world. Freud's aim in The Interpretation of Dream (1913) was to clarify that dreams express our latent desires. No other source for dream material besides the dreamer's experience. The dream differs from the experience as it tends to be more symbolic. The mind links and arranges information symbolically.

Dreams are symbols, and thus, called "interpretation".

Psychology acknowledges that dreams hold significance and can be interpreted, regardless of spiritual beliefs. Dreams are nonsensical when compared to neuroscience. Modern neuroscientists think that dreams are a byproduct of neurological processes. Dreaming helps our hippocampus encode information into long-term memory. The brain functions in its lowest frequency, known as delta, during sleep. Theta waves in the brain activate certain regions to induce neurological alterations. The connections between sensations, emotions, and memories in our mental function are made by the "cables". All humans exhibit these three fundamental aspects when any neurological process occurs. We only dream when it occurs. Dreams are random visions with no interpretable meaning, as per neuroscience. As humans, we have a habit of assigning significance to everything.

The dream's three perspectives can cause confusion. Sciences capture truth. Between these two sciences, which one do you rely on, regardless of your spiritual beliefs? Consider these points to help you decide.

Psychology and neuroscience both define dreams as internal and personal experiences. Have you ever dreamt of someone? Have you ever experienced precognitive dreams? Have you ever had a dream about a loved one, and then they contacted you the next day to express a need for your help or to say they miss you?

If someone dreams about losing their upper teeth, it may indicate that a male family member is unwell and may pass away soon. Your response will be proven despite your lack of knowledge about his family. Perhaps unaware, but will eventually find out. What is his source for this "message"? How does his subconscious anticipate the future?

Additionally, how would you respond if you encountered these? Psychologists and neuroscientists classify it as accidental.

Why can I control or navigate my dreams during lucid dreaming if they are a random neurological process? Any skilled lucid dreamer is capable of performing this task. The next chapter will discuss/address this issue. Let's conclude the dream discussion.

Each theory has its own scientific explanation to eliminate any confusion. It gets confusing when we attempt to take one and shove another. To fully comprehend the dream, consider these approaches: spiritualism, psychology, and neuroscience.

Dreams are caused by neurological processes in the brain or body. Brain processes lead to the generation of thoughts. The synaptic tracks of the brain link the regions accountable for thoughts, emotions, and sensations.

Psychology and neuroscience interpret the dream at different levels. At a functional level, people tend to see a dream spiritually. The psychology-neuroscience divide regarding dreams resulted from ignoring our ability to control the process. We can consciously dream and control our dreams. It is normal for consciousness to awaken during the dreaming state.

We usually dream randomly. At times, we recall our last night's dreams, but generally, we cannot. We may remember some of the faces and places in our dreams from last night, but not all. We've realized the neuroscience dream with this sign. Remembering your dreams vividly may be due to the lingering emotions in your body upon waking up. This is a dream of psychology. If your dream has a meaningful message and it comes true, it is your spiritual dream.

What about dreaming of others and it comes true? One question remains.

Today's people find this part hard to accept. I'll share my experiment to give you the answer.

I instructed two students to sit six meters apart and face each other. I made them both dream. I told them to feign sleep. In their induced sleep, I guided them to dream that one of them to draw a picture on the paper that I provided. In his dream, the student gave the picture to his friend by walking towards him. His friend was motivated to dream of getting the picture. I rouse them. I requested the recipient of the dream to sketch what was given by his friend on the paper. I asked the first student to draw his dream before verifying the picture. Next, they present the documents. They draw an identical picture. I did this with various students, both familiar and unfamiliar. The outcome was 80% success.

How could they have the same dream information if dreams are personal experiences? Only one theory can explain this. It is Quantum Physics. Quantum physics addresses consciousness, vibration or energy, and parallel worlds, although it does not specifically mention dreams. Remarkable! Dreams can convey distant information to us. Not discussing telepathy now; may do so in future books. You can dream of someone else and gain insight because we are all interconnected.

In quantum physics, our mind extends beyond our physical brain. Our brain wave carries coded thoughts and is transmitted through an invisible antenna. We are always broadcasting. If we transmit thoughts on different frequencies, we won't be able to communicate, similar to a radio tuned to a different station. We need to be on the same frequency before we can connect.

We exist within a vibrational or frequency ocean. Empty space is not devoid of entities. Empty space is not equivalent to nothing. It facilitates the connection. It is both intelligent and conscious. The term 'universal consciousness' originated today. If you find it hard to accept, as I told you earlier, the explanation can seem strange and nonsensical.

Quantum physics findings relate to ancient experiences of prophets and shamans. Quantum physics is the science of spiritualism in this case. Throughout history, we have been recognized as Prana, the energy expressed in physical form. At the sub-atomic level, we are pure energy according to quantum physics. Matter is the embodiment of energy, rather than mere storage of energy, as per Einstein's renowned equation $E=MC2$. Energy's omnipresence enables you to dream of someone else. You receive information about your friend because you are connected to them. You would have been chosen as blessed in ancient times, but not daily.

The subconscious communicates symbolically through dreams. The subconscious mind is a mode of consciousness, in addition to being a part of our mind. The gateway to alternate dimensions. Not all holographic images in your mind's darkness are illusions. Your subconscious mind receives a symbolic or coded message. Your subconscious mind uses an unfamiliar language to communicate with you. Your conscious mind converts it into language. Symbols can come in various forms, typically as images. Sometimes it is interpreted as imagination. Not all images require imagination. The subconscious mind interacts with us in that way. The subconscious communicates with us through emotions or physical sensations. A dream is what we call it when it occurs during sleep.

A dream springs from the unconscious (Freud preferred this term to subconscious). But the unconscious mind is not just a storage place. That is where the invisible antenna, energy control panel, and doorway to the other realm are situated.

The dream is clearly complex. Our brain continually processes information, and the mentioned neurological processes happen even when we rest. But we don't dream every time we sleep. We don't have pleasant dreams or bad dreams every night. Most believe that dreams occur every night but remain forgotten upon awakening.

With dedicated training, nightly lucid dreaming is achievable. Lucid dreaming can be utilized for interdimensional travel at an advanced level. But I won't discuss the astral projection, it's not a lucid dream anymore. A lucid dream is the optimal gateway to astral projection.

www.ingramcontent.com/pod-product-compliance
Lightning Source LLC
Chambersburg PA
CBHW050249120526
44590CB00016B/2271